Francis Frith's
England in the 1880s

Photographic Memories

Francis Frith's
England in the 1880s

Maureen Anderson

First published in the United Kingdom in 2001 by
Frith Book Company Ltd

Hardback Edition 2001
ISBN 1-85937-331-3

British Library Cataloguing in Publication Data

Francis Frith's England in the 1880s
Maureen Anderson

Frith Book Company Ltd
Frith's Barn, Teffont,
Salisbury, Wiltshire SP3 5QP
Tel: +44 (0) 1722 716 376
Email: info@francisfrith.co.uk
www.francisfrith.co.uk

Printed and bound in Great Britain

Front Cover: Dunster, Market House and Castle 1880 15837

AS WITH ANY HISTORICAL DATABASE THE FRITH ARCHIVE IS CONSTANTLY BEING CORRECTED AND IMPROVED
AND THE PUBLISHERS WOULD WELCOME INFORMATION ON OMISSIONS OR INACCURACIES

Contents

Francis Frith: Victorian Pioneer   7

Frith's Archive - A Unique Legacy   10

England in the 1880s - An Introduction   12

Harbours, Ports and the Seaside   15

Towns and Villages   54

Buildings   77

Cities   96

Index   131

Free Mounted Print Voucher   135

Francis Frith: *Victorian Pioneer*

FRANCIS FRITH, Victorian founder of the world-famous photographic archive, was a complex and multi-talented man. A devout Quaker and a highly successful Victorian businessman, he was both philosophic by nature and pioneering in outlook.

By 1855 Francis Frith had already established a wholesale grocery business in Liverpool, and sold it for the astonishing sum of £200,000, which is the equivalent today of over £15,000,000. Now a multi-millionaire, he was able to indulge his passion for travel. As a child he had pored over travel books written by early explorers, and his fancy and imagination had been stirred by family holidays to the sublime mountain regions of Wales and Scotland. 'What a land of spirit-stirring and enriching scenes and places!' he had written. He was to return to these scenes of grandeur in later years to 'recapture the thousands of vivid and tender memories', but with a different purpose. Now in his thirties, and captivated by the new science of photography, Frith set out on a series of pioneering journeys to the Nile regions that occupied him from 1856 until 1860.

Intrigue and Adventure

He took with him on his travels a specially-designed wicker carriage that acted as both dark-room and sleeping chamber. These far-flung journeys were packed with intrigue and adventure. In his life story, written when he was sixty-three, Frith tells of being held captive by bandits, and of fighting 'an awful midnight battle to the very point of surrender with a deadly pack of hungry, wild dogs'. Sporting flowing Arab costume, Frith arrived at Akaba by camel seventy years before Lawrence, where he encountered 'desert princes and rival sheikhs, blazing with jewel-hilted swords'.

During these extraordinary adventures he was assiduously exploring the desert regions bordering the Nile and patiently recording the antiquities and peoples with his camera. He was the first photographer to venture beyond the sixth cataract. Africa was still the mysterious 'Dark Continent', and Stanley and Livingstone's historic meeting was a decade into the future. The conditions for picture taking confound belief. He laboured for hours in his wicker dark-room in the sweltering heat of the desert, while the volatile chemicals fizzed dangerously in their trays. Often he was forced to work in remote tombs and caves where conditions were cooler. Back in London he exhibited his photographs and was 'rapturously cheered' by members of the Royal Society. His reputation as a

photographer was made overnight. An eminent modern historian has likened their impact on the population of the time to that on our own generation of the first photographs taken on the surface of the moon.

Venture of a Life-Time

Characteristically, Frith quickly spotted the opportunity to create a new business as a specialist publisher of photographs. He lived in an era of immense and sometimes violent change. For the poor in the early part of Victoria's reign work was a drudge and the hours long, and people had precious little free time to enjoy themselves. Most had no transport other than a cart or gig at their disposal, and had not travelled far beyond the boundaries of their own town or village. However,

by the 1870s, the railways had threaded their way across the country, and Bank Holidays and half-day Saturdays had been made obligatory by Act of Parliament. All of a sudden the ordinary working man and his family were able to enjoy days out and see a little more of the world.

With characteristic business acumen, Francis Frith foresaw that these new tourists would enjoy having souvenirs to commemorate their days out. In 1860 he married Mary Ann Rosling and set out with the intention of photographing every city, town and village in Britain. For the next thirty years he travelled the country by train and by pony and trap, producing fine photographs of seaside resorts and beauty spots that were keenly bought by millions of Victorians. These prints were painstakingly pasted into family albums and pored over during the dark nights of winter, rekindling precious memories of summer excursions.

The Rise of Frith & Co

Frith's studio was soon supplying retail shops all over the country. To meet the demand he gathered about him a small team of photographers, and published the work of independent artist-photographers of the calibre of Roger Fenton and Francis Bedford. In order to gain some understanding of the scale of Frith's business one only has to look at the catalogue issued by Frith & Co in 1886: it runs to some 670 pages, listing not only many thousands of views of the British Isles but also many photographs of most European countries, and China, Japan, the USA and Canada — note the sample page shown above from the hand-written *Frith & Co* ledgers detailing pictures taken. By 1890 Frith had created the greatest specialist photographic publishing company in the world,

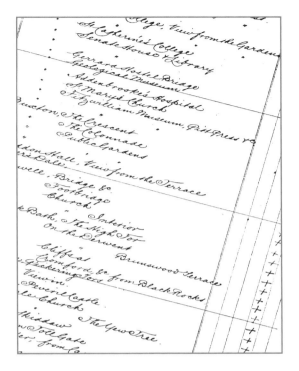

Frith's death, a new card measuring 5.5 x 3.5 inches became the standard format, but it was not until 1902 that the divided back came into being, with address and message on one face and a full-size illustration on the other. *Frith & Co* were in the vanguard of postcard development, and Frith's sons Eustace and Cyril continued their father's monumental task, expanding the number of views offered to the public and recording more and more places in Britain, as the coasts and countryside were opened up to mass travel.

Francis Frith died in 1898 at his villa in Cannes, his great project still growing. The archive he created continued in business for another seventy years. By 1970 it contained over a third of a million pictures of 7,000 cities, towns and villages. The massive photographic record Frith has left to us stands as a living monument to a special and very remarkable man.

with over 2,000 outlets – more than the combined number that Boots and W H Smith have today! The picture on the right shows the *Frith & Co* display board at Ingleton in the Yorkshire Dales. Beautifully constructed with mahogany frame and gilt inserts, it could display up to a dozen local scenes.

Postcard Bonanza

———

The ever-popular holiday postcard we know today took many years to develop. In 1870 the Post Office issued the first plain cards, with a pre-printed stamp on one face. In 1894 they allowed other publishers' cards to be sent through the mail with an attached adhesive halfpenny stamp. Demand grew rapidly, and in 1895 a new size of postcard was permitted called the court card, but there was little room for illustration. In 1899, a year after

Frith's Archive: *A Unique Legacy*

FRANCIS FRITH'S legacy to us today is of immense significance and value, for the magnificent archive of evocative photographs he created provides a unique record of change in 7,000 cities, towns and villages throughout Britain over a century and more. Frith and his fellow studio photographers revisited locations many times down the years to update their views, compiling for us an enthralling and colourful pageant of British life and character.

We tend to think of Frith's sepia views of Britain as nostalgic, for most of us use them to conjure up memories of places in our own lives with which we have family associations. It often makes us forget that to Francis Frith they were records of daily life as it was actually being lived in the cities, towns and villages of his day. The Victorian age was one of great and often bewildering change for ordinary people, and though the pictures evoke an impression of slower times, life was as busy and hectic as it is today.

We are fortunate that Frith was a photographer of the people, dedicated to recording the minutiae of everyday life. For it is this sheer wealth of visual data, the painstaking chronicle of changes in dress, transport, street layouts, buildings, housing, engineering and landscape that captivates us so much today. His remarkable images offer us a powerful link with the past and with the lives of our ancestors.

Today's Technology

Computers have now made it possible for Frith's many thousands of images to be accessed almost instantly. In the Frith archive today, each photograph is carefully 'digitised' then stored on a CD Rom. Frith archivists can locate a single photograph amongst thousands within seconds. Views can be catalogued and sorted under a variety of categories of place and content to the immediate benefit of researchers.

Inexpensive reference prints can be created for them at the touch of a mouse button, and a wide range of books and other printed materials assembled and published for a wider, more general readership - in the next twelve months over a hundred Frith local history titles will be published! The day-to-day workings of the archive are very different from how they were in Francis Frith's time: imagine the herculean task of sorting through eleven tons of glass negatives as Frith had to do to locate a particular sequence of pictures! Yet

See Frith at www. francisfrith.co.uk

the archive still prides itself on maintaining the same high standards of excellence laid down by Francis Frith, including the painstaking cataloguing and indexing of every view.

It is curious to reflect on how the internet now allows researchers in America and elsewhere greater instant access to the archive than Frith himself ever enjoyed. Many thousands of individual views can be called up on screen within seconds on one of the Frith internet sites, enabling people living continents away to revisit the streets of their ancestral home town, or view places in Britain where they have enjoyed holidays. Many overseas researchers welcome the chance to view special theme selections, such as transport, sports, costume and ancient monuments.

We are certain that Francis Frith would have heartily approved of these modern developments in imaging techniques, for he himself was always working at the very limits of Victorian photographic technology.

The Value of the Archive Today

Because of the benefits brought by the computer, Frith's images are increasingly studied by social historians, by researchers into genealogy and ancestory, by architects, town planners, and by teachers and schoolchildren involved in local history projects.

In addition, the archive offers every one of us an opportunity to examine the places where we and our families have lived and worked down the years. Highly successful in Frith's own era, the archive is now, a century and more on, entering a new phase of popularity.

The Past in Tune with the Future

Historians consider the Francis Frith Collection to be of prime national importance. It is the only archive of its kind remaining in private ownership and has been valued at a million pounds. However, this figure is now rapidly increasing as digital technology enables more and more people around the world to enjoy its benefits.

Francis Frith's archive is now housed in an historic timber barn in the beautiful village of Teffont in Wiltshire. Its founder would not recognize the archive office as it is today. In place of the many thousands of dusty boxes containing glass plate negatives and an all-pervading odour of photographic chemicals, there are now ranks of computer screens. He would be amazed to watch his images travelling round the world at unimaginable speeds through network and internet lines.

The archive's future is both bright and exciting. Francis Frith, with his unshakeable belief in making photographs available to the greatest number of people, would undoubtedly approve of what is being done today with his lifetime's work. His photographs, depicting our shared past, are now bringing pleasure and enlightenment to millions around the world a century and more after his death.

England in the 1880s - *An Introduction*

ENGLAND HAS AN area of approximately 50,000 square miles, just over half the entire area of the United Kingdom. The North Sea's mighty breakers wash the east coast and the Irish Sea ebbs and flows onto the northwest coast. The south coast has the English Channel and the south-west corner juts out into the Atlantic Ocean. Nowhere in England is further than 75 miles from the sea.

On the 28 June 1838, Alexandria Victoria, at the young age of 18, was crowned Queen of England in Westminster Abbey. She was to be the longest ruling monarch in British history, 64 years in total. Born in 1819, she lived until 1901, through almost the entire 19th century, a time that saw more changes to the country than any previous century.

Victoria was not a particularly clever woman, but she had, throughout her reign, loyal and very able Cabinet ministers. Her first prime minister was Lord Melbourne and he took it upon himself to be father and secretary to her. He educated her in politics and gave her the grounding that was later to make her influence very strong.

Victoria married her first cousin, Prince Albert, in 1840. Theirs was a truly happy marriage and they had nine children. In 1861 Albert died and the Queen became a virtual recluse hiding away at Windsor, Osborne House on the Isle of Wight and Balmoral Castle, avoiding London whenever possible. Because of this disappearance from the public eye, she was nicknamed 'the Widow of Windsor'. Towards the end of her reign she once again became more publicly involved with the people and on her Jubilees the entire population of the country celebrated, with villages and towns being decorated with bunting and lights, street parties and ceremonies.

The decade before the 1880s had brought the introduction of compulsory elementary education and a law which prevented children under ten from working. Prior to this, most boys had some basic

literacy skills, but very few girls had any form of education other than the trade in which they were employed. These included domestic work, glove or lace making, which was usually done in groups or 'schools', and straw plaiting which was often carried out in the home by children as young as five. Following the passing of the Education Act, girls also learned to read and write, although some parents were reluctant to lose one of their breadwinners.

Another major change was a decline in agriculture and farming. By 1874, many tenants had given up their farms because of bad weather, poor harvests and low prices, which in turn affected many landowners who relied on rents from their tenant farmers. Many of the farmers moved to the cities to work in the industries that were becoming a major part of the economy. By 1881 there were as few as one in ten employed in agriculture while the manufacturing industries accounted for 30% of the working population. This meant that the landowners and aristocracy had to make a living elsewhere and many turned to investments and to directorships within the cities. The railways were constructing branch lines from all the main lines as mining, shipping and other major industries reached commercial prosperity. The owners of these enterprises were newly wealthy and socially ambitious.

The 1880s saw a huge increase in the population, even though many families emigrated to the Dominions and the United States. Musical culture and the arts took on a new importance. The Guildhall School of Music was founded in 1880, The Royal College of Music in 1883 and operas were produced and orchestras formed.

For hundreds, if not thousands of years, the ports and harbours were the only lines of communication to anywhere beyond the shores of Britain. The coastline determined the livelihood of many. Fish and shellfish provided food and the means to trade. Later, as more exploration took place and new worlds opened up, the smuggling of tobbacco, geneva (gin) and other commodities not readily available, became rife, especially on the more rugged coastline where caves provided hiding places, and hidden inlets provided the means for boats to come ashore away from the prying eyes of the preventitive men. Sadly, shipwrecks also provided the more unscrupulous with a bonus to their income. The 'wreckers' would watch a vessel break up on the rocks or founder in the heavy seas, and once what remained was within reach, would pounce and carry off anything that was useable or saleable.

The 19th century brought vast changes. Smuggling was in decline by the 1820s as a more efficient coastguard came into existence and the risks for the smugglers became too great. Although there were still vast numbers of shipwrecks, there were more and more lighthouses being erected, and towards the later part of the century lifeboats became more sturdy and safe. The medieval harbours that had once been used to transport the things that were vital commodities, such as wool and corn, were improved or rebuilt. Mining had reached its peak in the 18th century and carried on to the 19th, so the southern ports became busy with, among other natural resources, the export of tin, copper and china clay, and the northern ports with alum and iron ore. The fishing industry expanded and some of the harbours housed large fleets of trawlers. The railways arrived from the mid- 19th century onwards and slowly but surely branch lines made their way to the coastal villages and towns. For the fishing industry this was a real boon as it meant the fish could be packed in ice and sent to all corners of Britain to arrive sooner and therefore fresher. Cod from Hartlepool, herring from Staithes and Flamborough and pilchards from Cornwall would be served up in the best hotels in London. The railway, although a godsend to many, meant a gradual decline in the use of the smaller ports. At first many of the trains were for goods only but passenger trains soon followed which meant that most of the coastal towns and villages found an income from a new source - the tourist!

The factory workplaces of the Victorians were cramped, noisy and extremely unhealthy. Their living accommodation was often in back-to-back houses and to have space for a garden was rare. By the 1870s it became law that the workforce had half a day off on Saturday. Now they had spare time and the railways gave them a faster means of transport than the horse. These two factors opened up a whole new world for them as they invaded the seaside areas. They could board a train with their families, which they did in their thousands, and go to the seaside to get away from the smog and drudgery of their workplaces and the towns. By the 1880s, the towns and villages that had once relied solely on fishing and trade had now become adept at catering for the holidaymaker. The buildings in the coastal villages were usually small cottages, catering only for the families of fishermen. Hotels and lodging houses were needed for visitors, so large Victorian buildings jostled for space alongside the small cottages on the sea fronts and around the ports and harbours. The locals found employment as hoteliers, waiters, kitchen hands, laundresses and the like. Thankfully, many medieval, Tudor, Georgian and Victorian examples of architecture have survived, especially in the southern regions of England, and stand together in a harmony that can still be pleasing to the eye.

The last half of the 19th century brought changes in fashion. The middle classes were now sharing the country's general prosperity and could afford to be a little more fashion conscious. Ready-to-wear garments and a wider choice of fabrics were becoming available due to the technical advancements in textile production. To the Victorians, as well as a break from routine, a day out gave the opportunity to show off their finest clothes. Men's apparel was usually dark, loose-fitting suits until 1885 when well-cut lounge suits became popular. Headwear consisted of top hats for formal occasions and boaters and bowlers for informal. Little boys were often dressed in sailor and knickerbocker suits and the older boys in breeches. Girls wore many layers of frills and dresses protected by pinafores, while the ladies really made an impact. Their styles were feminine and colourful but very uncomfortable to wear. Tight lacing showed off a trim waist and the bustle made a return to become the height of fashion around 1885, but then disappeared forever in 1889. Sports and holiday clothes for different activities soon became available - although not always very suitable in design. Because they were loose-fitting and much more comfortable, especially on a warm day at the seaside, they soon took over from the tight corsetry and heavy layers of skirts and petticoats previously worn.

This collection of images from one decade within the 19th century shows: a time when simple activities gave a great deal of pleasure; architecture was magnificent - if a trifle austere; unsurpassed feats of engineering - bearing in mind the comparatively primitive equipment and tools then available; the sailing ships which plied the ocean and opened up communication and trade with other countries; and the simple working folk, such as fishermen.

The streets, that once rang with the cries of street hawkers and beggars, the clop of horses' hooves and the rattle of the trams, now hum to the noise of modern day traffic. Ladies skirts have risen from ankle length to mini and the sombre suits of the gentlemen have become jeans and jogging pants. However, although so many changes have come about, our Victorian ancestors have left their mark on our cities, towns and villages and their monuments can still be seen amidst the ever-changing views.

Harbours, Ports and the Seaside

Accommodation and a decent beach were not the only requirements needed to attract the visitor. In the past the wealthier classes who had spent time at the seaside had been quite happy with shell collecting, horse riding, walking, bowls and perhaps quoits; but now something more stimulating was required - and was provided. Fishermen would use their boats to take the public on fishing trips, while others converted their boats to give pleasure tours. Horse-drawn cabs were always lined up along the promenades ready to take individuals or families on sightseeing trips around the immediate vicinity, and bicycles were readily available for hire for those who wished to view the area whilst partaking of light exercise. Some areas had spa baths and hydropathic establishments, which were popular, as sanitation was still very basic within the home.

Amusements were set up on the beach: donkey rides, swings and roundabouts for the children; Punch and Judy, which appealed to all generations (an entertainment hardly seen now because of domestic violence being such a public issue); and brass bands, palm readers, refreshment rooms and photographic stalls for the adults. They all contributed to a day out to be remembered as a real treat when the time came to travel back to an often very hard daily existence.

Intrigue was a favourite with the Victorians, making villages that had been used for smuggling, such as Polperro in the west, interesting places for them to visit. The narrow streets, with little houses overlooking tiny harbours, fed the imagination. Saltburn, on the north-east coast, was once just a hamlet on the shoreline, until New Saltburn was built higher

up on the cliff. John Andrews was the landlord of the Ship, one of the inns in the original hamlet, and was notorious for carrying out the illegal trade. Eventually the revenue men managed to catch and imprison him.

The Victorians loved piers, they were places to see and be seen, and they were erected in almost every resort, sometimes by the Corporation and sometimes by private funding from a wealthy local family or landowner. Often, as well as being used for landing stages for boat trips, they had bandstands, seating and sometimes pavilions built on them. Some were simple affairs but many were very grand. Kiosks on the landward end, selling souvenirs and buckets and spades, were a must. Some of the kiosks were used as toll booths, as there might be a charge for the pleasure of a walk along the pier. Sadly, many are now gone, due to erosion from the sea, fires, ships driving into them during storms, causing massive damage, and the lack of finances to repair and maintain them. The Chain Pier in Brighton was the first to go in Britain. Closed in 1896, it collapsed in a storm shortly afterwards.

The larger steam boats began to take over from the smaller vessels, both for boat trips, and fishing. Because the larger boats caught such large quantities of fish, the industry for the smaller fishermen went into decline. Sailing and fishing vessels became more modern and motorised and the ports and harbours became the home of pleasure boats instead of the working vessels. Now, instead of the little fishing cobles and the rigging and sails of the tall ships, yachts and motorboats dominate the waterfronts.

The rivers were also a popular attraction. There was nothing that families liked better than to cruise around on water dressed in their best. Rowing boats, houseboats, punts and steam launches would crowd together on the rivers so the water could hardly be seen. Most of the river ports and harbours have a strong link with a medieval past, and many of them are still bustling with export and import in the present day. Some have acted as defences against invasion from the sea, and often very successfully too!

Clockwise from top left: details from images 20237, 20318, 21080 and 19369

◀ **Padstow, The Harbour 1888** 21214
This very ancient port has long been associated with trading and shipbuilding. In the Middle Ages, silt formed the Doom Bar and cut off the harbour for the larger sailing vessels, but it still continued to be a very important trade port. Tied up at berth, the sails of this vessel are perha drying out.

◀ Newquay, The Sands 1887 20237

A harbour wall was built here as far back as 1440 and the present harbour was built in 1838. The area became busy when a goods railway was opened in 1874 to transport china clay. When a passenger railway followed in 1876, it brought with it the Victorian holidaymakers who wanted to enjoy the surf and the clean white sands.

▼ Padstow
The 'Sunbeam' 1888

21217

On North Quay is a bench called the 'Long Lugger', which is the meeting place for the town's 'old boys'. Here they sit chatting and watching the pleasure craft and fishing boats - all very different from the scene a century ago, when this type of sailing vessel with its intricate rigging would have dominated the port.

◀ Charlestown
The Harbour c1885

16771

This port was designed in the 1790s for the landowner Charles Rashleigh by John Smeaton, who was a famous harbour engineer. When first planned it was to be an outlet for tin, but was soon taking china clay from the diggings nearby. The larger docks of Par eventually took over the trade.

▼ **Fowey, The Town Quay 1888** 21250
On the right is the Working Men's Institute established in 1868, next to it is the
King of Prussia Hotel and on the left is the Bonded and Ship's Store. It advertises
General Grocery and Italian Warehouse, French Bread made to order and
Handmade Ships' Biscuits. A lone child sits on the harbour wall watching the camerman.

▼ **Looe, Quays 1888** 21311
East Looe and West Looe are set on the steep banks of the River Looe
and are connected by a bridge over the harbour. Until the 1880s, they
were separate towns. Cornish granite, including the stone that was
used to build Westminster Bridge, was shipped from here.

▲ **Polperro, The Harbour
1888** 21270
Built in a narrow gully in
cliffs 400 feet high, this
was once a smuggling
village. Many of the
fishermen's cottages
looking onto the harbour
were built in three
storeys, the ground floor
being used for storing
and salting their catches
of fish. The living quarters
and bedrooms were
reached by an exterior
flight of stone steps.

◄ **Plymouth
Mount Edgcumbe 1889**
22385
The westernmost seaport.
The waterfront looks onto
where Devon meets
Cornwall and five rivers
mingle into Plymouth
Sound. The Mayflower
sailed for the New World
from here in 1620 with the
Pilgrim Fathers. Francis
Drake, Captain Cook and
other seafaring legends also
set out from here on their
epic voyages.

**Plymouth
George Street 1889**
22397
The circular building on the left is the offices of the Great Western Railway; the town clock is in the centre. As can be seen by the cabs and horses and carts it was once a very busy street. Sadly, along with much of Plymouth, it was virtually destroyed during the Second World War.

◀ **Dartmouth**
Battery Point 1889
21589
The two castles on opposite sides of the river mouth were built towards the end of the 15th century to guard against French attack. These were the first in England to be designed especially for artillery. The castle to the front of the view is at Kingswear. The distant castle is now open to public viewing.

◄ **Plymouth, Union Street 1889**
22359
The street linked the towns of Plymouth and Stonehouse. On the right there are Turkish Baths and on the far corner is Octagon House which had 'good beds and tea, coffee and cocoa at a penny a cup'. Near the pharmacy roof is an advertisment for James Dome's black lead and above the door one for Pearl Sanitary Soap - an odd combination!

▼ **Dartmouth Dittisham On the Dart 1889** 21617
Until the sailing vessels were diverted to Southampton, the Dart was a very busy waterway with sea-going vessels carrying merchandise and mail to and from the busy port of Dartmouth. The river is now used mainly for leisure and water sports.

◄ **Dartmouth Dartmouth Regatta 1889** 21648
Still very much a sailing town, the Royal Regatta, which is held annually in August, still attracts huge crowds. Of course, nowadays the craft are quite different to the sailing vessels in the photo. The social life within the yacht clubs and the river attract many naval officers to live out their retirement here.

**Totnes
Fore Street 1889**
21628
The street climbs up from the River Dart, passes under the medieval East Gate and then becomes High Street. The church of St Mary in the distance was built in the 15th century. By their stance it looks as though the gentlemen may have been asked to pose for the camera. Notice that except for one little girl, there are no women on the street.

◀ **Torquay
Fishermen 1888** 21445
The village was the
supply depot for the
British fleet during the
Napoleonic Wars. Many
of the families of the
seamen took up
residence here so they
could spend more time
with their menfolk. The
Mediterranean weather
attracted people in ill
health, especially
suffering from
consumption, which was
very common in the
19th century.

◀ Paignton
The Pier 1889 21529

This was one of the many seaside villages in Devon that owed its expansion to the coming of the railway in 1859. The pier was constructed in 1879 but it caught fire in 1919 and has been rebuilt.

▼ Torquay, From Walden Hill 1888 21420

Looking towards Vane Hill, this image was taken before the outer harbour was built in 1900. Along the base of Walden Hill is Torbay Road which was laid out in the 1840s. The houses here are mainly 19th-century. The limestone and permian cliffs along this coast are host to many small inlets and beaches.

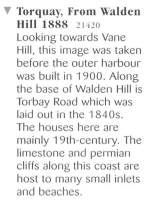

◀ Minehead
The Harbour 1888
20888

Many Victorian buildings were erected to cater for the holidaymakers who flocked here every summer to enjoy the very wide, firm sands. The town developed by importing Irish wool for the Taunton weavers. In the background is North Hill which shelters the harbour from the easterly winds.

Ryde
The Pier c1883 16297
The steamer is berthed at the second longest pier in England with its passengers waiting for the last of the luggage to be lifted on board by the small crane. The crowds stand outside the refreshment rooms ready to wave goodbye to family and friends as they set out for the mainland.

Weston-super-Mare The Sands 1887 20318 Swings, Punch and Judy, and to the left, the Castle Coffee House Refreshment Tent, all served to attract the visitor to this seaside resort. People do not dress up in their finest clothes for the beach nowadays, but one thing that has not changed is the fact that entertainments then, as now, would have you dipping into your purse.

◀ **Rye**
West Cliff 1888 21145
A terrible storm in 1287 changed the course of the River Rother and brought prosperity to Rye with it becoming a trading port. Eventually silt blocked off the sea channel and the town turned to fishing and smuggling to survive. Perhaps the crew of the sailing ship have gone for a jug or two at the Anchor Inn on the hill.

◀ Clifton, The Bridge 1887

20167

The Suspension Bridge joins Clifton and Leigh Woods above the Bristol Avon. The bridge was begun in 1831 but due to lack of finance was not completed until 1864. Built with 1,500 tons of steel salvaged from London's Hungerford Bridge, this was a marvellous feat of Victorian engineering.

▼ Rye, West Street 1888

21159

Rudyard Kipling stayed at Lamb House which is at the top of this cobbled street. His 'Smuggler's Song' was written about Rye. The house was host to George I in 1726, then in 1899 it was bought by the American author Henry James and was the setting for his work 'The Turn of the Screw'.

◀ Folkestone Harvey Statue 1887

19963

The statue was erected in 1881 as a memorial to Dr William Harvey who, in 1628, discovered the circulation of the blood. The outstanding architecture of the houses shows the wealth that sustained this area. Wheelchairs became the modern equivalent of the bathchair that is parked by the railings.

Margate, View on the Jetty 1887 19700
The jetty was opened in 1855 but was demolished by storms in 1978. Until the railway arrived in the 1840s, thousands of holiday makers would travel from London over the waters of the Kentish Flats and land at the end of the stone pier that encloses the harbour and which was built about 1815.

Margate, The Beach and Bathing Machines 1887 19869
A Quaker glover from Margate, Benjamin Beale, invented the bathing machine. These caravan-shaped contraptions would be pulled out a short way into the sea by horse, to allow bathing with privacy and decorum. They had gone into decline by the early 1920s when bathing tents became used instead.

Broadstairs, York Gate 1887 19726
Here, where Charles Dickens wrote 'Bleak House' and 'David Copperfield', there has been little change. The gate, which looks onto the harbour, was first built by George Culmer in 1540, and rebuilt in 1795. Originally it was known as Flint Gate and was renamed after the Grand Old Duke of York.

▼ **Broadstairs, North Foreland Light 1887** 19728
Built in 1875, this is believed to stand on the site of an earlier lighthouse of 1505. The beam from the light could be seen from 20 miles out to sea. The pretty cottage was built as accommodation for the lighthouse keeper; to the right of the view is a flagpole.

▼ **Ramsgate, From West Cliff 1887** 19674a
In 1748 there was a violent storm from which every vessel in the vicinity sought shelter, many of them in the small harbour at Ramsgate. Because of the protection it afforded, within the year a new harbour was being built. In this view, many of the Regency buildings are in use as hotels.

▲ **Herne Bay, The Parade and Clock Tower 1889** 22313
The clock tower was a gift from Mrs Ann Thwaytes, who stayed here during the summer in the 1830s; the opening ceremony was in 1837. The free-standing clock is believed to be one of the earliest in the country. Prior to 1971, when an electric motor was installed, the mechanism was hand wound. One winder, Alfred Smith, performed the task from 1847 to 1907. In 1905 during renovation work, a builder was crushed by a clock weight which fell through two floors.

◀ **Lowestoft
Entrance to Harbour
1887** 19838
Fishing has been the main
source of livelihood for the
people here since the 16th
century. The harbour was
improved in the 1840s
because of a danger from
silting. The little boats have
now been replaced with
large fleets of trawlers that
find fish by using sonic
equipment.

New Brighton
The Fort 1886 14269
The fort was constructed in stone between 1826 and 1829
to defend Liverpool from coastal attack. Not in use now, the
lighthouse was erected between 1827 and 1830. Both are now
listed buildings. A metal drum acts as a buoy and bobs up and
down along with the rowing boats on the calm sea.

New Brighton
The Beach 1887 20067
On the sands in front of the fort, along with the roundabouts and swings typical of the seaside resorts in Victorian times, a new attraction, a photographer, has set up stalls. J and A Ansonia would have done well recording the visitors' days out, as very few families would have owned cameras.

Morecambe, The Pier 1888 21080
Here we can see a group of gentlemen, including one on a two wheeled 'cycle' pose at the pier entrance. In its heyday the pier, built in 1869, had a ballroom and was the busiest place for entertainment for miles around. The pier was demolished after a devastating fire in 1991.

**Bridlington
The Quay and
Harbour 1886** 18041
Situated in a natural
break in a line of cliffs,
the quay was once
separate from the rest
of Bridlington. The
harbour walls are mid-
19th-century and
replaced medieval piers.
Most of the buildings
here which cater for the
holidaymaker were
erected between 1850
and 1880.

**Flamborough Head
North Landing 1886**
18001
The villagers wait with
their baskets for the
boats to come in with
their catches of herring.
In the middle of the
19th century there
were 30 fishing boats
here, but they had all
gone just after the First
World War. The
treacherous seas here
have claimed many lives
and hundreds of
seafarers are buried in
the graveyards.

Scarborough Bay 1886 18240 A magician entertains a crowd of well-dressed Victorian holidaymakers on the beach. The town has been popular for centuries, once as a spa town known as the 'Queen of Watering Places' - a healthy, bracing and fashionable resort. The town has a mixture of architecture, with the ruins of a 12th-century barbican and keep, and Regency and Victorian buildings.

▼ **Robin Hood's Bay, 1886** 18195
Crammed together on higgledy-piggledy streets that drop down towards the sea, the houses suddenly give way to the large open area at the shore. The last two centuries have seen many buildings lost to the erosion of the cliffs. In the early 19th century the village prospered with its catches of herring. The tools of the fishermen; lobster pots, a fishing coble and sets of oars are scattered up the steep bank. A storage shed outside a cottage is reached by a set of precarious steps.

▼ **Whitby, The Harbour 1885** 18168
This view is taken looking north across the harbour. High on the hill are the abbey ruins and over to the left, the lovely Norman church of St Mary. The church is reached by a climb of 199 steps that leaves one breathless. The official name for the stairs is Church Steps, but they are known locally as Jacob's Ladder.

▲ **Whitby
Queen Ann's Staithe
1886** 18167
Captain Cook lived here for nine years learning sailing skills. His two ships that sailed to the South Seas, the 'Resolution' and 'Endeavour', were built here. In Victorian times many of the Whitby men were engaged in whaling, for which they had to sail far out to sea.

◀ **Staithes, The Harbour c1885** 18215
The young James Cook was apprenticed to a Staithes grocer and, listening for hours to the fishermen's tales, he became so fascinated by a life on the ocean, he ran away to Whitby where he signed on as a cabin boy which was the beginning of his later famous career. Fishing is still very much a part of Staithes, just as it has been for centuries.

▼ **Staithes, The Bridge 1886** 18208
This view is hardly changed today except that the bridge is a much more sturdy replacement and the fishermen do not use it now for hanging their nets. The winding cobbled streets, the cottages that seem to lean on one another, and the overall picturesqueness is now an attraction for artists and sightseers.

▼ **Saltburn-by-the-Sea, From Coastguard Path 1885** 18104
In 1884 a water balance cliff lift was built here to save the long climb down from the village to the lower promenade. It is now the oldest surviving working lift of its type in Britain. The pier has just undergone a £2m restoration to return it to its original Victorian glory.

▲ **Hartlepool East from Ferry Landing 1886** 18840
Just behind the little ferry terminal is the Coal Exchange Hotel. The Commissioner's Ferry, which was established in 1854, was essential transport for the hundreds of men who worked at the shipyards and engine works at Middleton. Old Hartlepool, as it is known, is rich in history and there have been many important archaeological finds here.

◄ Redcar, High Street 1885
18134
To the left is the ornate drinking fountain which was knocked over and demolished by a car in 1922. No cars here though, just a horse and cart and gypsy caravan trundling up the wide road. To the right at No 107 is C Bell's Ready Money Drapery Establishment. He advertised 'a special selection of hats, bonnets, flowers, feathers, infant's millinery and general millinery'.

**Redcar
The Esplanade 1886**
18131
With Redcar Pier in the background, two gentlemen sit chatting among their bicycles for hire. Horses and carriages wait to take families on a sight-seeing tour along the sea front. The bathing machines, which were introduced here in the 18th century by Charles Turner, a landowner, are dotted around the beach. The lady on her three-wheeler looks quite at ease pedalling along.

Redcar
The Sands 1886 18133
Gentlemen, perhaps
fishermen, sit at the
side of a coble watching
the children
approaching the
donkeys and their
masters. If the children
have a ½d they will be
able to have a ride up
and down the beach. In
the background the pier
can just be seen; the
small gabled building to
the right of the view is
the lifeboat house.

Towns and villages

For generations, villagers had relied on farming and agriculture for their livelihood and land would have been passed down to them, father and son. For many, the severe agricultral depressions of the 1870's and 1880's meant an end to this way of life, and others, who had managed to survive those severe years, later lost the battle, unable to keep up with changing farming practice. The drift of people to the industrial centres continued and the population of villages became much reduced - but they survived.

In many cases the best survivors are those villages built by local landowners for their estate workers. In modern times, especially with really beautiful villages, they have been taken over by organisations such as the National Trust and English Heritage, and so remain virtually as they were built. One such village is Cockington with its pretty thatched cottages, 14th-century forge and a mill wheel that still turns. Another is Selworthy, also with thatched cottages and a large 14th-century church. Many of the early villages were built around large green areas that were used as common land for grazing livestock and for village gatherings. The green in Bainbridge is one that has survived along with an age old custom of blowing a bull-horn to bring the foresters home. West Burton also has a green, which was once the setting for market fairs, selling mainly wool, and Wensleydale cheese made by monks at nearby Jervaulx Abbey.

The regular markets, however, were held in market towns. Before the advent of shops, markets were the only means by which the locals could sell and trade their wares, and market days could be quite grand occasions. The many market towns of England all have their particular charms and many have remnants of their medieval origins. Ancient churches, market crosses and castles testify to past wealth. Dunster, for example, overlooked by an ancient castle, attracted merchants to buy the local cloth, Dunsters, which was of excellent quality and very strong, and Kendal, now known as the gateway to the lakes, established the wool industry in 1331. By the 1880's, however, although markets were still popular, shops had a strong foothold and the beginnings of the modern day chain stores were evident. The Victorian shop fronts were often very elaborate, and many of the wares would be on display on the pavement outside.

As transport became available to the working classes, the Victorian visitors arrived in droves, by rail, coach and steamers to the peaceful and grandiose scenery of the lakes, much as to the seaside. The fresh, clean air and the wooded hills provided a welcome respite from the factories and mills of Lancashire. This influx of visitors shattered much of the peace. As new hotels and boarding houses sprang up, the waters of Windemere and the neighbouring lakes became alive with ferries and steamboats and on the jetties brass bands played. Thankfully, the magnificent scenery has changed little from the the way it was described in many of Wordsworth's works.

In the latter part of the 19th-century, England saw

a strong revival in the popularity of drinking, and bathing in spring water - believed to be a cure for all sorts of complaints. Buxton had attracted visitors since Roman times for its warm water spa, and when the railway arrived in the late 1800s it experienced a revival as a spa town. The Palace Hotel was built to accommodate the visitors arriving by rail, and there was also the Octagon, an entertainment centre, the Pump Room and Solomon's Temple, a folly that was erected to give work to the unemployed. The coming of the railway

also had an impact on Bowness, which had been a tiny village, but then suddenly mushroomed with the opening of the Hydropathic Hotel which offered remedial bathing.

Many memorials were erected to Queen Victoria for her Golden Jubilee in 1887, and her Diamond Jubilee in 1897. Mainly in the form of drinking fountains, statues and town clocks, a large proportion of these survive today, in pride of place in the main street of our towns.

Clockwise from top left details from images 17885, 20484, 15837 and 21088

Cockington
The Village 1889 21539
When the Cockington estate was to be split up, the Prudential
Building Society - whose staff had been evacuated to the village
during World War II - invested in the estate and so the village has
been preserved. Tourists now come in horse-drawn carriages from
Torquay to visit this picturesque area.

◄ **Dunster**
Market House and Castle
c1880 15837
The original castle was built before 1086, but after many changes, its present appearance is due to reconstruction in the 1860s. The Yarn Market Cross was built around 1589, and to the left was a town house, which by 1880 had become a hotel. Except for traffic, the scene today is very much as it was over a century ago.

◄ Selworthy, 1883
15836
The old gnarled trees add character to this idyllic setting which is Selworthy Green, now owned by the National Trust. The thatched cottages were erected in 1828 by Sir Thomas Dyke Acland for his retired estate workers. Many of the cottages have survived, retaining their original charm.

Sherborne ►
The Conduit
1887 19669
Once used by the Benedictine monks, the Conduit was moved to this site in 1539 after the Dissolution of the monasteries. The street is Cheap Street, the main shopping area for the town. In the distance can be seen the tower of Sherborne Abbey.

◄ Taunton, St Mary's
Church 1888 20858
The tower of St Mary Magdalene was rebuilt in 1862, copying very closely the first church, built around 1500. Leading to the church, Hammet Street, laid out in 1788, survives almost as it originally was except for the buildings on the left which have given way to a modern office block.

◀ **Leatherhead
The Clock Tower 1888**
21343
This was built in 1869 to house the horse-drawn fire engine, previously kept in a church. The building later became a public toilet and was then demolished in the early 1950s. The clock was given by the Congregational Chapel because they could not afford to keep it when a tax was levied on public clocks.

Sherborne South Street 1887
19670

Dating from the 8th century, the town is situated on the north bank of the River Yeo. The buildings are mainly Georgian, Regency and Victorian. Sir Walter Raleigh built a castle here in 1594. More recently, in the 1960s Sherborne was the setting for the musical film 'Goodbye Mr Chips'.

Leatherhead, The Swan Hotel 1888
21342

The Swan was a 17th-century coaching inn where horses were changed between London and Brighton. The Moore family ran the inn for generations from about 1850; they also established a brewery, the offices being where the tree is in the photo. The brewery closed about 1922, and the inn was demolished in 1936 to make way for Burton House, erected by Burton's Tailors. The swan emblem above the portico survives in the town's museum. The corner shop on the right has also gone and a large curved building, now National Westminster Bank, is in its place.

Reigate Suspension Bridge 1886 18968a

The iron bridge was erected in 1825 to span a cutting that had been made through the chalk to widen and straighten the road. It was replaced in 1910 by a concrete structure. The young gentleman wheeling his bicycle up the hill has stopped to doff his cap to the gentry on the coach while two women watch from the bridge.

Reigate
West Street 1886 18958
This view is looking from High Street towards Dorking. Most of the
houses were demolished in the early 20th century for road-
widening purposes. To the rear of the view on the left, the Blue
Anchor Inn survives, as does the large house on the right with
twin chimneys, now in use as a dental practice.

Reigate
Vanderbilt's Coach Venture 1886 18968b
The two young chaps have stopped to talk to the ladies in the buggy at the rear of the large coach. The party, dressed in their finery with the ladies wearing their large flowery hats, are on an outing on a coach owned by the millionaire, Alfred Gwynne Vanderbilt. His fortunes stemmed from his family's involvement in the expansion of New York. Although his interests were in banking and railways, his great love was coaching and his coach travelled daily to and from Brighton. He died on board the Lusitania when it sank during the Great War.

Dorking, High Street 1888 21324
There has been little change to this part of the street except for some of the shop fronts being slightly modernised, the names changing, and, of course, the modes of transport. The building to the right front of the view is gone, but Attlee, who occupied the premises and were corn merchants, still trade at the old mill in the town.

▼ **Bletchingley, The Village 1886** 18980
An early market town, Bletchingley's fortunes depleted towards the end of the 16th century. Development began again in the 19th century, but the village managed to retain some of its medieval charm. The cottages on the right still exist. The largely 15th-century church of St Mary had a reredos added in 1870 among other Victorian additions.

▼ **Buxton, The Gardens 1886** 18659
A peaceful scene of ladies playing tennis, their mode of dress very different to the short skirts and teeshirts of today. The tennis courts gave middle class females the chance to indulge in an affordable sport and to make new friends, including suitable men as it was an acceptable mixed-sex sport.

▲ **Matlock Bath
The Footbridge 1886**
18611
The sign on the end of the beautiful latticework bridge across the Derwent advertises 'High Tor Recreation Grounds' and 'This way to the Fern Cave Lover's Walks and Switzerland View'; it sounds very romantic. The handcarts on the left seem to have been abandoned, perhaps the owners are on the Lover's Walks!

◀ Buttermere
The Village 1889 22057
A little-known hamlet before
the age of the motor car,
the surrounding woodlands,
fields and nearby lakes now
attract walkers. The
immediate scenery has
changed very little in
centuries. The small parish
church of St James
overlooks Buttermere Lake
and peaceful farm buildings.

**Kendal
Stricklandgate 1888**
21088
Many of the buildings
were constructed from
grey limestone, hence it
being known as 'the
auld grey town'. Near to
the confectioner's
barrow are the Kendal
Auction Rooms, and
outside on the footpath
a lady with a parasol
looks on as a young girl
wheels a tot in a three-
wheeled pram out onto
the road.

◄ **Keswick
The Bridge and Greta
Hall 1889** 22086
Greta Hall, beyond the
bridge over the River
Greta, was lived in by
Samuel Coleridge in
1800. Later his brother-
in-law, Robert Southey, a
Poet Laureate, lived
there for 40 years until
1843. The building on
the river bank advertises
'A Banks, Pencil Works'.
The Pencil Factory is
now on the other side of
the bridge.

Buildings

England is rich in buildings from medieval to Victorian, and all the many different types of architecture that came between, each having its own beauty and character; visitors now come from all corners of the world to view the wealth of historical buildings that are in every county of Britain. It was in the 19th century when a real interest in England's history and heritage began. The Victorians carried out major restoration work on churches, cathedrals and houses. Industrialists and landowners built large ostentatious dwellings and filled them with works of art. Some houses are still occupied by the families who have had them for generations, such as Haddon Hall in Derbyshire and Wilton House in Wiltshire. Many are now open to the public, not just to help with the enormous cost of their upkeep, but because their owners take pride in showing off the splendour of these stately homes. Others have become tourist attractions, museums, homes for the elderly, public offices or schools - such as Canford Magna which opened as a boy's school in 1923 but now caters for girls as well. The buildings often stand in many acres of land and some have beautiful, well-preserved gardens, many of them terraced and full of the plants that were popular in times gone by.

Some buildings have had many changes of use, such as Lowestoft which was originally called Fairfield House; the name was changed in tribute to the architect who designed it. In 1882 the building was enlarged and over the years it has been in service as a convalescent home, a Church Army hostel, accommodation for the YMCA, and is now apartments. There was also a period of ten years when it lay derelict. The magnificent Crescent in Buxton has also had a variety of uses, including a clinic in the 1930s. Part of the building is now apartments and part the Tourist Information Office. Lancaster Town Hall has been the premises of banks, and extensions to it have been used by the police and the fire service.

As long as there has been a use for these fine buildings, whatever it may have been, it has assured their survival.

Gothic architecture was popular throughout the Victorian era and was often used in remodelling and renovation - as in Place House at Fowey in Cornwall, Wilton House and many of the churches and cathedrals.

Sadly, some buildings have disappeared either through bomb damage during the wars, the march of progress or because of the lack of finance for their upkeep - such as the Hydropathic Establishment at Baslow in Derbyshire. Written records and photographs are often all that remain of these great buildings.

Clockwise from top left details from images 21071, 20204, 19797 and 18649

St Columb Major
Glebe House and Church 1888 21194
This is part of a larger Elizabethan hall house that was built in the
late 16th century and belonged to the parish church. In 1895 it
was sold by the rector of the church and became a boot shop. It is
now in use as tea rooms. The 15th-century church has had a
series of mishaps. In the 17th century, three boys lit gunpowder in
the church; the boys were all killed and the cost of the damage
was £350. In 1895 a meteorite damaged the tower and the church
has also been struck by lightning.

Fowey, Place House 1888 21254
Originally medieval, and added to in Tudor times, the house was later restored by Joseph Treffry, a Victorian Industrialist, with the roofscape and towers in Regency Gothic. There are the most elaborate carvings in wood and stone, both inside and out.

Fowey, The Drawing Room of Place House 1888 21255
The typical decorative taste of a wealthy Victorian: heavy drapes, ornate fireplace and ceiling, heavily patterned carpet and wallcoverings, and large chandeliers dominate the room. Beautiful ornaments, photographs and objects fill every available shelf, complimenting the slender, often tapestried chairs.

Fowey, The Lugger Inn 1888 21252
Many ancient buildings have survived on the steep narrow streets of this old town, including this inn which was a 17th-century hostelry. Fowey, pronounced to rhyme with 'toy', has one of the best natural harbours on this part of the coast, and in the Middle Ages this was an important port between the Continent and Ireland.

▼ **Fowey, The Ferry Inn, Bodinnick 1888** 21236
This little town is built on a steep hill on one side of Pont Creek, an estuary of the
Fowey River. From here, the ferryboats would take the passengers across to Fowey.
Daphne Du Maurier, the famous authoress stayed here when still a young girl and
often lunched with her parents at this quaint inn.

▼ **Poole, The Town Hall 1887**   19506
Note the elegant staircase leading to the first floor of this Georgian Town Hall, built
in the 1700s. In use as a museum for a time, it is now the home of the town's
branch of the local history society. The Crown and Anchor still serves a pint under
the same name, but sadly the ornate sign has disappeared.

▲ **Poole**
The Town Cellars 1887
19511
Some parts of the ancient
cellars date from 1300.
Known as the King's
House, or the
Woolhouse, it was used
in medieval times to store
wool before export. It is
now a museum for Poole
Pottery. The tall building
with the gabled roof,
which was Oakley's Mill,
is now the Waterfront
Museum.

◀ **Canford Magna Manor c1886** 19490
In 1825, this impressive large house was added to the remaining medieval great hall that is known as John of Gaunt's Kitchen. The house was owned by the Winbournes. The manor and its 300 acres of grounds were sold by Viscount Winbourne, and in 1923, a school was founded which is still in use today.

Wilton, Wilton House and The Italian Gardens 1887 19806

The Earls of Pembroke have held this land since the Dissolution of the monasteries. Much of the house was rebuilt in the 17th century, after a fire all but destroyed the building. The Gothic hall and cloisters were completed in the 19th century. The house is full of works of art and the gardens are a joy to view.

Stonehenge, 1887 19797

An epic feat of prehistoric technology, bearing in mind the way they are put together and that the stones were brought from miles away. Trying to find the origins and significance of the stones has captivated historians, archaeologists and laymen for centuries.

Brighton
The Pavilion 1889
22245

Originally a Palladian building, the Pavilion was remodelled in 1815 for the Prince Regent, later to become George IV, who was a regular patron of Brighton. The pierced stone latticework, domes and columns with an Indian flavour were designed by the architect John Nash. The interior is full of fantasy creatures in bright colours.

◄ **Ashbourne, Green Man 1886** 18577
These two inns, the Green Man and the Blacks Head Royal Hotel, were built in 1750. The two are now one hotel, keeping the title Green Man. On the top of the 'gallows' sign, as they were known, are the faces of Blackamoor: one side is smiling and the other scowling.

**Buxton
The Crescent 1886**
18649
The 5th Duke of
Devonshire
commissioned John
Carr, a noted architect,
to design somewhere
for visitors to stay. This
elegant Georgian
building was the result.
The Great Stables were
erected behind and
later covered with a
massive slate dome.
When it was built in
1881 it was the largest
dome in the world.

▼ **Via Gellia, Tufa Cottage 1886** 18586

At one time this charming cottage was a gamekeeper's residence. Still lived in, it has survived virtually unaltered. The title Tufa comes from the name of the unusual local stone used in its construction. Perhaps the lady on her pony and trap was the owner at the time this photograph was taken.

▼ **Lowestoft, The Convalescent Home 1887** 19856

The convalescent home was a gift to the town in 1877 from William Birbeck, who was himself ill and died in 1897. Here some of the staff and patients are having a game of croquet on the front lawn while others look on, perhaps enjoying the benefits of a sunny day.

▲ **Southport, Cambridge Hall and Bank 1887**
20204
Much of the land here has been reclaimed, as the sea receded and left sand dunes. Many of the principal buildings, such as banks, are on Lord Street pictured here, which was laid out in 1825 and extended in 1854. Southport is a popular residential area for people who work in nearby Liverpool.

Baslow
The Hydropathic
Establishment c1884
16582

Known as the Hydro, this impressive building with over 100 bedrooms was built in 1880. Spa baths and treatments were popular as a cure 'for all ills' and this establishment offered excellent facilities. Declining custom and high running costs led to closure in 1930 and in 1936 the building was demolished.

◄ **Rowsley**
The Peacock Inn 1886
18617
Originally built as a manor
house for John Stevenson
1652, this building later
became the dower house
Haddon Hall, the seat of th
Duke of Rutland. It also
served as a farm for a time
and in about 1820 becam
a hotel. The stone peacoc
above the door is taken
from the Duke's family cre
- hence the name of the in

Haddon Hall
The Entrance Tower
1886 18630
Now held by the Duke of Rutland, the hall's beginnings were in the 12th century. Unlived in from 1740 for nearly 200 years, sympathatic restoration began in 1912, taking some 20 years to complete. In the last century it was used as a location by film producers.

Grantham
The Town Hall 1889
22286
The Guildhall was built by William Watkins of Lincoln and was completed in 1869 at a cost of £2,480. The Newton Memorial was designed by William Theed and was inaugurated in 1858. Although the statue survives, sadly it succumbs to occasional vandalism.

Boston
The Church 1889
22269
This was the port from which a group of Puritans left for America in 1630 to later found Boston, Massachusettes. The statue is of Herbert Ingram who founded the 'Illustrated London News' in 1842 and was an MP here. He drowned in 1860. The tower of St Botolph's Church is known as the Boston Stump.

◀ **Beverley
St Mary's Church
West Front c1885**
17887
The church was built
with the backing of the
medieval guilds in the
12th to 16th centuries.
The tower was rebuilt
after the original
collapsed and killed
some of the
worshippers. This
church stands at one
end of the town and
at the other is the
twin-towered
Beverley Minster.

Bowdon
Parish Church 1889 21917

The church of St Mary the Virgin was built between 1856 and 1860, mainly of materials salvaged from other buildings. A cabman's shelter is placed conveniently outside the church so that the cabbies could sit in comfort while waiting to take the worshippers home after the sometimes lengthy services.

Worsley
Court House 1889 22267

Built in 1849, the half-timbered Court House is a very impressive Tudor 'copy'. The village, which is now surrounded by motorways, still retains a lot of its history. There is the church of St Mark, built by Sir Gilbert Scott in 1846, and the Bridgewater canal which was completed in 1803 to carry coal from the mines.

Lancaster
The Town Hall 1886
18091

Town Halls and Tollbooths have stood on this site from the 12th century. This building was erected between 1781 and 1783 but has been added to in later years with many extensions. The urns on the parapets were removed in 1952 because they were unsafe. A new Town Hall was completed in 1909 and in 1923 this building became a museum.

Heysham
St Patrick's Chapel Ruins, Heysham Head 1888 21071
Sited on a cliff and on ground that slopes steeply on the north and west
sides, it is believed the chapel is of Anglo Saxon origin. In the immediate
vicinity many rock-cut graves have been discovered, some dating back
to 900AD. The ladies are sheltered from the sea breezes by the ruins.

Nappa, The Hall 1889 21665

A rather odd name to call a building as Nappa means 'turnip patch'. This is a rare survival of a fortified farmhouse that was built in about 1460, the seat of the Metcalfe family. In 1556 Christopher Metcalfe was Sheriff of York and formed a bodyguard of 300 men, all in uniform and on horseback.

Kirkleatham, The Hospital c1885 18137

Sir William Turner Hospital was built in 1676 as almshouses. The Georgian Chapel was added in 1740 by Cholmley Turner in memory of his great uncle William whose death mask is displayed within. The building has been in use and lived in since its beginnings, serving for a time as a school.

The Cities

The population explosion in London in the 19th century was unprecedented, helped along by almost a million migrants descending on the city. Over 30% were classed as poor and many resorted to begging, stealing or confidence tricks just to survive. Poverty breeds crime and, early in the century, nowhere was it more rife than here. When transportation of criminals to America ceased, prisons had to be built. These included Brixton, Pentonville and Holloway and punishment was harsh. By the 1880s, however, the crime rate had dropped considerably although in 1888 the notorious Whitechapel murders took place - attributed to the faceless 'Jack the Ripper'.

Many of the poorer classes took up trades, however menial, to try and give themselves and their families relief from the never-ending struggle against poverty. Because of the increase in population new forms of transport were provided including horse buses, railways and trams. This meant that those who could afford the fares could move to the outer suburbs, while the poor remained in the inner city within walking distance of their work, and so new 'social classes' came to be. Many of the older buildings were subdivided to form flats and with overcrowding and overpricing these areas became slums. Throughout the 19th century urban expansion continued and London spread to cover a huge area.

Changes to markets began, conditions became less insanitary and the little craft shops became the early chain stores that have marched up the streets making them into the popular shoppers' paradise they are today. The heart of London developed

from a busy, jostling mercantile and trading centre to become the commercial and financial centre of the Empire. Headquarters were built to house the new banks and insurance companies.

Two other cities, hot on the heels of London, were Liverpool and Manchester. Liverpool was once just a tiny fishing village until, early in the 18th century, the busy port of Chester was cut off because of the Dee silting up. Chester's loss was Liverpool's gain; by 1880 it had become a city and one of the biggest ports in the world. Expansion continued when the tunnel under the Mersey was completed in 1886. The docks, with its huge warehouses, stretched for eight miles along the river. Manchester became a city in 1853 by Royal Grant, its chief trade being clothing. It led the way in both transport and free trade and is still one of the main shopping areas in England.

Other cities owe their status to their rich history: Canterbury, Salisbury, Chester, Winchester (once the capital of England, beginning in Saxon times)

Ripon and York. Many of their abbeys and cathedrals were restored during the Victorian era, some of the restorations were, sadly, not very sympathetic, but at least these grand churches have survived. Other places, such as Bristol, became large and wealthy because of overseas trading from the ports. Bath was very fashionable as a spa town in the 18th and 19th centuries, but had attracted visitors since Roman times to seek a tonic, a cure or refreshment with its warm, natural spring water.

During the wars the larger towns were targeted and, sadly, many of the Victorian buildings, and sometimes whole streets, were lost to bomb damage. However, many of these grand buildings, erected in a conspicious display of an affluent society, did survive. An increase in public awareness and conservation laws will, hopefully, ensure their survival as a memorial to an age when industry and commerce in England took the world by storm.

Clockwise from top left details from images L130110, 12684, 20001 and L130330

Bath, The Abbey, West Front 1887 19583
The Abbey was built in 1499, on the site of a cathedral that had been left to decay after a fire. There are 52 windows making the interior exceptionally light, thus the description 'the lantern of England'. On each side of the door are the two Saints, Peter and Paul to whom the Abbey is dedicated. Above the door is a statue of King Henry VII. On each side of the stained glass window can be seen the wonderful stone carving of two ladders, up which figures are endeavouring to climb to heaven – with varying degrees of success!

Bristol, Temple Church 1887 20129
Situated on Church Lane, the church was founded in around 1147 by the Knights Templar. Some of the remains of the present church date from the 1390s. The tower, which is 114 feet high, leans at an angle due to age and subsidence. The Shakespeare Inn on Victoria Street, to the front of the view, is now a listed building.

Bristol
The Quay 1887 20133
The tall ships were a common sight here in the 17th and 18th centuries. It was in Bristol that trade between Britain and the New World began. Tobbacco was imported here and African slaves were carried on Bristol ships, known as Bluebirds, to the West Indies to work on the plantations.

Salisbury
The Cathedral and Palace 1887 19733
The spire is the tallest in the country and the setting probably the most handsome. Painted and photographed so often, it is familiar to many. The interior is light, airy and at the same time awesome, with its beautiful stone columns reaching towards the spectacular fan vaulting.

Salisbury, Poultry Cross 1887 19786
A copy of Chichester's Cross, Poultry Cross was used by preachers to give their sermons and as a place to sell produce and is mainly 14th century. Through the arch of the Cross, carts can be seen carrying milk churns. Behind the buildings is the tower of St Thomas Becket Church.

Brighton, The Aquarium 1889 22238
The brainchild of Eugenius Birch, the Aquarium has been a popular tourist attraction since it was first opened in 1872. The clock tower and gateway were added in 1874 and many other additions followed. In 1889, a licence was granted for the live performance of dramatic plays.

Maidstone, Market Place 1885 12684
The drinking fountain, with its statue of Queen Victoria, was given to the town by local banker Alexander Randall and was erected in 1862 at the top of the High Street, on the old market site. The building beyond the fountain was originally the market. Built in 1762-63, it then became a police court and later the town hall.

Canterbury
The Cathedral 1888 21357
Architecturally very intricate, and set at different
levels, this is the most significant of all the English
cathedrals. Early French Gothic, Romanesque and
Perpendicular styles - all can be seen in the fabric
of the building. Thomas Becket was murdered here
during vespers and his body was laid to rest
within the cathedral.

Winchester
The City Cross 1886 19443
The cross stands on a very plain plinth and is one
of the oldest forms of market place decoration. The
building to the rear houses Gartlands, selling
furniture, china, glass, cutlery and plated goods.
A sign above the shop advertises the Great Western
Railway Agents, A W White and Co, household
removal contractors.

London, Match Seller 1884 L130116
The young, barefoot and undernourished-looking boy is selling Bryant and May's Alpine Vesuvian matches, made in London and commonly known as Brimstones. Sometimes these children were sent out to work or to beg by their families, but all too often they were orphans for which begging was the only means of survival.

London, Ginger Cake Seller 1884 L130111
The thick slabs of cake, made with treacle, flour and ground ginger, were thoroughly enjoyed by the Victorians.
The pieces were put into paper cones and a blanched almond was placed on the top.

London
A Hokey Pokey Stall, Greenwich 1884 L130110
A smiling youth, a stall keeper and a dandy gent
pose for the camera, along with the ragged
children eating their treats of a penny ice-cream.
Behind are billboard stickers advertising an estate
agents and 'South Eastern's London to Brussels,
Short Sea and Mail' and 'Cheap Trips
to the Sea-Side'.

London
Sweep 1884 L130115
The older men were the Master Sweepers and they
employed young boys, and sometimes girls, to
climb the chimneys using their elbows. These
children usually had a short life span. In 1875 the
practice of using children became illegal and the
invention of George Smart - hollow chimney rods
with a bristle brush - were used instead.

London, Nomads 1885 L130212
The nameless, faceless gypsies came and went, selling their wares wherever they travelled. There would be rich pickings in London. The working classes were very superstitious and, although wary of the gypsies, their curiosity would get the better of them and they would pay to buy the wares or have their palms read.

London, Whitechapel Road 1885 L130214
At a stall full of tools, chains and cartwheels, a young boy watches as the man plies his trade on a manual grinder.
Perhaps the boy has been sent on an errand to have a household or butcher's knife sharpened, or perhaps he is
watching because he will one day take over the stall.

London
The Royal Exchange 1886 L130012
This photograph was taken on the Square Mile, right in the heart of the
financial area of London. The wealthy merchants arrive by carriage and
the bowler-hatted professional traders walk between the Exchange, the
Bank and their offices. Commerce is still frantic here today, the only
difference being that technology, in the form of computers, mobile
phones and faxes, save on shoe leather. The two chaps at the front of
the view have other things on their minds, one carries what is perhaps a
cupboard door, and the other seems to have a tennis racquet.

London, Hyde Park c1890 L130330

This is the largest green area in central London. It was originally one of Henry VIII's deer parks and was primarily used for hunting. The park was opened to the public in the 17th century. Here, on Rotten Row, the fashionable and the elegant mingle to gossip and show off.

London, The Houses of Parliament 1886 L130188

Most of the original medieval palace, built about 1365, burnt down in the great fire of 1834. Only Westminster Hall and the Jewel Tower survived; the rest was rebuilt in the neo-Gothic style. This huge building has more than 1,000 rooms.

**London
King William Street
1880** L130102
This photograph shows the junction of Cannon Street and the approach to the new London Bridge, which was named after and opened by King William IV in 1831. In 1844 a statue of the King was erected to the right of where this view ends. Because of the increase in traffic the statue was moved to near Greenwich Hospital.

London
Whitehall 1880

L130016

In 1738 a new road was created. Parliament Street was intended to improve the entrance to Whitehall, but judging by the horses and people here, a lot more room was still needed to avoid this bottleneck. In the early 1900s the road was widened, which eased this sort of congestion.

**London
Old Houses and
Staple Inn c1886**
L130174
On the kerbside, in the centre of the photo, is a stone obelisk which is the remaining one of two that marked the City boundary. At this time the stucco had recently been removed from the frontage of the Staple Inn, revealing the beautiful Elizabethan half-timbering. The bookshop advertises '3 in the Shilling, Discount Office'.

◀ **London**
Piccadilly Circus 1886

L130186

This area was very much altered when, in 1885, buildings were demolished to make way for a new street, Shaftesbury Avenue. The pillared building to the right is the newly-built London Pavilion Music Hall and the statue of Eros stands proudly in the centre forefront of the view.

▼ **London, Cheapside**
c1886   L130066

In this view, looking east, we can see on the left the Manufacturing Company of Singer Sewing Machines. The three passengers chat away as their horse-drawn vehicle is driven by a gentleman in a top hat. This area has totally changed, as it was rebuilt after bombing in the Second World War.

◀ **London**
Great Northern
Railway Station c1886

L130067

Although the surroundings have altered, the terminus of the Great Northern Railway in King's Cross remains virtually the same today. A rather plain edifice compared to most of the rather extravagant Victorian railway stations.

◀ **Chester
Eastgate Street 1888**
20594
The large building to the front of the view is Brown, Holmes and Co, silk merchants to Her Majesty and HRH of Wales. At the end of the view is the city wall which was built in 1769, replacing an earlier medieval wall, which in turn replaced a Roman wall. Eastgate was the Roman's Via Principalis.

◀ **Chester
The Cathedral, West
Front 1888** 20577
In the late 19th century
the cathedral was in a
dreadful state of disrepair
and Gilbert Scott was
commissioned to carry
out substantial
restoration work.
Although not as popular
with tourists as other
cathedrals because of its
Victorian restoration, it
has some pleasing
details, including a
13th-century chapel and
exceptional choir stalls
which are 14th-century.

Chester ▶
Watergate Street 1888
20608
The carcasses of
chickens hang outside a
butchers' shop so
customers can inspect
before they buy. Above
are the premises of
Maddocks, a cabinet
maker and upholsterer.
No veneer here, solid
wood furniture was
hand-crafted and made
to last.

◀ **Chester, Bridge Street
1888** 20599
Bridge Street and
Watergate Street meet at
The Cross and are lined
with what are known as
the Rows. These are
mainly black and white
timbered buildings, such
as the one in this photo
- some medieval and
some remodelled by the
Victorians. They have
shops on walkways at
first floor level.

**Liverpool
The Exchange 1887**

20001

A busy stock market day. Liverpool was second only to London as a trading centre. Two of the men are holding bales which could be cotton samples, as this was the main outlet for the Lancashire cotton trade. This was a man's world only, note the absence of any females.

◀ **Manchester**
The Cathedral 1889 21868
Dedicated to St George, St Mary and St Denys and built in the 15th century in the Perpendicular Gothic style, it was given cathedral status in 1847. Inside is glorious carved woodwork, particularly on the choir stalls, from the 16th century. A tower was added in 1868 which greatly enhanced the cathedral's appearance.

◄ **Liverpool**
St George's Plateau
c1881 14071
Queen Victoria and Prince Albert ride large bronze horses which stand among other Victorian monuments. St George's Hall, to the left, was designed in 1836 for social events and to house the Courts of Justice. It was described as the 'greatest Greco-Roman building in Europe'.

▼ **Manchester**
The Royal Infirmary
c1885 18256
The cabs are lined up in the middle of the road waiting for fares, while the street sellers ply their wares on the kerbside outside this impressive building which was to be demolished in the early 1900s. The site was then used for a temporary library before becoming Piccadilly Gardens.

◄ **Manchester**
The Exhibition, Royal
Entrance 1887 21901
The cabs and trams would have been busy ferrying people to and from the Royal Jubilee Exhibition at Old Trafford, which attracted thousands of people. A temporary building was erected to celebrate Queen Victoria's Golden Jubilee and was later demolished.

◀ **Leeds**
Fountain 1888 21003
Because of an observation
that there was no drinking
water in Roundhay Park, the
architect, Thomas Ambler,
was commissioned to
design a fountain. The result
was this elegant structure
with eight columns. It was
connected to the town's
water supply, providing
continuous refreshment
through 20 taps.

◀ **Manchester**
Market Street 1889
21899

The facade on the left is now the Arndale Centre. At this time the buildings to the front of the view are occupied by a printing office and Hunsworth oil refiners. The first tram is heading for Bellvue and Hyde Road and the second to Alexandra Park. Along the kerbside is a row of ornate gas lamps.

Bradford ▶
The Town Hall 1888
21007

The Gothic building was opened in 1870 by the Mayor, Alderman Mark Dawson. The title of the building changed to City Hall in 1965, which was thought to be in keeping with Bradford's importance. The Titus Salt Memorial was erected in 1874 outside the Town Hall but was later moved to Lister Park because of traffic congestion.

◀ **Bradford**
The Council Chamber
1888 21009

Many changes have taken place to the Town Hall over the years. A new Council Chamber was incorporated into a large extension built in 1909. In 1914 the main staircase was redesigned and the area that had been the Council Chamber was reconstructed.

◀ **Ripon**
The Cathedral Library
c1885 18338
Although the smallest in England, the cathedral is nonetheless awe-inspiring. The library dates from 130(? and was originally the Lady Chapel. The bookcases pictured here are numbere(with Roman numerals. The library's collection of books and manuscripts from the 12th and 13th centuries are now looked after at Leeds University. Theology studen(and societies use this librar(regularly for study and meetings.

◀ **Harrogate, 1888** 20922

Overlooking The Stray, (the name stems from the cattle and sheep once roaming there) on the right of the view is the Prospect Hotel. The town became famous for its spa water and in 1842, when the Royal Pump Room opened, thousands of visitors flocked to the town. Consequently many large hotels were built.

York ▶
The Minster, South West c1880 12894
This magnificent building was completed in 1472, and in the 20th century underwent vast repair and restoration. The pride of the city, its towers can be seen towering above the other buildings. It has 128 windows and wonderful Gothic architecture, woodwork and stained glass. Even though it is now a cathedral rather than a minster, it is still used for daily worship and has many thousands of visitors.

◀ **Ripon, The Cathedral South West and the Bridge c1885** 18318
In the shadow of the Cathedral is the River Skell, with the arched Bondgate Green Bridge. The building on the river bank was No 107, the last building in King Street. It was the workplace of Whitfield Benson, a whitesmith and bellhanger. This part of the river has now changed almost beyond recognition.

York, Stonegate 1886 18449

The sign stretching over the street advertises Boddy's Star Inn, which was at No 40. Boddy was a landlord in the 19th century and he died at these premises. The inn, which dates from the 17th century, still survives, but is much altered. The business' signs were known as 'gallows signs' and sometimes they were so low that passers-by would have to duck to pass beneath them. On the left, the shop sign advertises 'Waddington's Piano Forte Manufacturer'. At the side of the cobbled street the little boy dressed in breeches and beret stares with fascination at the cameraman.